Redwing

Redwing

Collected Poems by
Marvin Orbach

First Edition

Hidden Brook Press
www.HiddenBrookPress.com
writers@HiddenBrookPress.com

Copyright © 2018 Hidden Brook Press
Copyright © 2018 Ariella Orbach

All rights for poems revert to the author. All rights for book, layout and design remain with Hidden Brook Press. No part of this book may be reproduced except by a reviewer who may quote brief passages in a review. The use of any part of this publication reproduced, transmitted in any form or by any means, electronic, mechanical, photocopied, recorded or otherwise stored in a retrieval system without prior written consent of the publisher is an infringement of the copyright law.

Redwing
Collected Poems by Marvin Orbach

Editor – Richard Marvin Grove
Cover Design – Richard Marvin Grove
Front Cover Photograph – Richard Marvin Grove
Layout and Design – Richard Marvin Grove
Back Cover Memorial Poem – Chris Faiers

Typeset in Arial
Printed and bound in Canada
Distributed in USA by Ingram,
       in Canada by Hidden Brook Distribution

Library and Archives Canada Cataloguing in Publication

Orbach, Marvin, 1940-2015
[Poems]
    Redwing / collected poems by Marvin Orbach. -- First edition.

ISBN 978-1-927725-52-8 (softcover)

    I. Title.

PS8629.R37 2017   C811'.6   C2017-907070-3

Contents

Essay - Flying High and Low beside
        Marvin Orbach's *Redwing* – *p. 1*

Foreword – *p. 9*

Introduction – *p. 14*
What is Poetry? – *p. 15*

SPRING
What an Old Man Told Me – *p. 18*
Wishful Thinking – *p. 19*
Initiation – *p. 20*
Dalia – *p. 21*
My Mother is the Sun – *p. 22*
Victorious – *p. 23*
In Flamingo Park – *p. 24*
Ever So Softly – *p. 25*
Golden Spring Morning on my Naked Limbs – *p. 26*

SUMMER
Softly Falls – *p. 28*
A Rebirth – *p. 29*
A Piece of Sky – *p. 30*
For Every Damsel – *p. 31*
My Love – *p. 32*
To a Little Blue-Eyed Mexican Girl – *p. 33*
How to Deal with Time – *p. 35*
Coyuca Lagoon – *p. 36*
Forced Freedom – *p. 38*

AUTUMN
Ephemeral – *p. 40*
I Die Each Evening – *p. 41*
Redwing – *p. 42*
What Comes of Life – *p. 43*
Chicks Sent by Express Train – *p. 44*
To a Butterfly – *p. 45*
To Mr. N—— Who Does His Best in a Cartage Company – *p. 46*
A Pine Tree's Lament – *p. 47*

WINTER
Silverfish – *p. 50*
True Happiness – *p. 52*

A Short Biography of Marvin Orbach – *p. 54*

Flying High and Low
beside Marvin Orbach's *Redwing*

Dear Reader:

It was with much pleasure and reverence that I accepted the request by Richard Grove, Publisher of Hidden Brook Press, to write a foreword to Redwing, a provocative jewel of poems written by Marvin Orbach. The book was thoroughly and lovingly compiled by his daughter, Ariella.

As I stepped into the man and his work, the first thing that impressed me was that Orbach, known to be very modest, had never told anyone about his poems: it was his wife, Gabriella, who found them after his passing. Ariella herself said once that her "dad was very humble". That makes Orbach an even greater librarian, book collector, poet and person. His formidable legacy of books and his passionate poetry honorably contribute to the already vast Canadian cultural mosaic.

My usual approach to writing a foreword starts with skimming the work to get into the mood and style of the material. In the case of this book I changed that procedure as soon as I started reading by jotting down notes as I flipped through the pages outlining my first-read impressions. Orbach's book has been divided in the four seasons, in the order of Spring, Summer, Autumn and Winter. As a whole I found the book to be a fine collection of thirty poems whose center is light, sometimes witty critique about social issues, and nature.

Before setting Orbach´s wings free, I want to talk to you about the solid synergy of the book that makes it a singularly self-standing gem. The poet´s spirit transpires in ways that you will take notice of as you finish reading it, full. There is variety in theme, tempo and style in Redwing, and what such richness does is to contribute to the wholeness of the book. You can sense it; you can see it when you are lit by "**True Happiness**", the closing poem, and then you are carried back by the very bird to "**Introduction**", the opening one. You will enjoy the back-and- forth flight, I assure you that.

With this foreword I share with you my feelings about the poems as independent units. Each of them left an indelible imprint that accompanies me yet refuses to sit just there. So, I must pour that out with a critique of a number of the poems. Allow me on this journey.

The poem "**Introduction**" is Orbach´s showcase summary of his fondness for nature, which he describes with the depth of a connoisseur and the passion of a lover. You will be then confronted with the opposite in the next lines: Orbach´s disapproval of those who spoil the beauty of the scenes he has just depicted. The imparting of the poet's understanding to the "fools" is related to their being unable to see the harmony of natural life and act senselessly. To the poet, however, that reality has been revealed, and he will powerfully present it to those fools in his poetry.

In the poem "**What is Poetry**?", Orbach likens poetry to what he admires in nature. He swiftly moves with an emphatic enumeration of colours and sounds to stir the reader's senses, and finally blends into a tender metaphor of birds and human hearts. The last stanzas are overlapping metaphors of soft and sharp images. As a reader I was taken aback by his last line; yet it is his choice – the liberty he himself proclaims in the poem! – to use phrases that will stick with us long after we finish reading his book.

The first poem of the Spring section, "**What an Old Man Told Me**", confirms the poet's determination to openly state his feelings.

Orbach puts words in the voice of an old man, old age generally respected in present and ancient cultures, which would be too harsh coming from someone else's lips. On this apparent irreverence of expression Orbach mounts his criticism and waves the flag of generous nature.

Every man's secret longing surfaces in "**Wishful Thinking**". The surprise element in this frank poem is served to you in the crescendo repetition of What? The poem is straightforward: no beating around the bush.

In "**Initiation**" Orbach moves form idyllic themes to more direct, intimate ones. He sings to the act of living and enjoying life. He is worried about others having a "sour death"; and he definitely does not wish to be one of them. He sings to his urges and wishes to be accepted. Orbach's poem "**Dalia**" is simmering fire. I loved its movie-like depictions. The poet skillfully fuses the splendor of the meadow and the environment with the passion of love, sprinkled by poetic wording. "**My Mother is the Sun**" is a succession of metaphors that jump from inside the poet to the outside world beating around him.

Defied by things that weigh heavily on a human being, the poet remains a victor blessed by a "light of life". Yes, "**Victorious**" brings us a hymn to life. I wonder why Prometheus, the mythological character, came to my mind as I read this poem. The poet brought him to me; here Hercules is Orbach´s "light of life". Think about it!

With the thoughtful skill of a philosopher Orbach gives us a genuine metaphor: "In Flamingo Park"´s last stanza allows you to actually see grapevines move, "crash through the poet's skull" looking for the meaningful life out there that is the "sweet air of pregnancy".

Delightfully handled, "**Ever so Softly**" intentionally plays with the word "Softly" and uses synonyms for the verbs in the stanzas. The poet insists on the adverb that opens every stanza: do it softly, to revel in the offering. The biblical phrase "Seek and you shall find" comes to me with this poem. Orbach wants the reader to pause for a second, softly, and live in the peace that he builds with his words.

My studies on Canadian literature unveiled for me the profound, unavoidable connection of Canadian writers and poets with nature, specifically with their extraordinary, varied, precious landscapes and creatures therein. This is a recurring motif in them, and by extension in Orbach. "**Golden Spring Morning on my Naked Limbs**" joyfully reminded that to me. Through repetition, this time at the end of each stanza, Orbach lets you know that the character in the poem is receiving all this gratification. This is a poem of optimism and both physical and spiritual satisfaction.

"**Softly Falls**" is a sustained metaphor that Orbach masterfully compacts into a haiku-like structure where the woman is a garden, the man is the nourishing rain. I loved it, as I loved "**A Rebirth**", another well-embroidered metaphor that speaks of gratefulness. If you want to read a gifted writer compacting words into charming poems and elevating apparently down-to- earth objects to higher ranks, do not miss "**A Piece of Sky**" either.

A poem brought back to me the great English poetry of the 19th Century: I have always been a devoted follower of classic English poets. "**For Every Damsel**" is the first, and only, rhymed poem in the book. Rhyme pertinently adds to the incessant motion of the images unfolding before the reader's eyes. The explicit "hopes" and the implicit dreams the author proposes are key words.

"**My Love**" offers metaphors deeply and irrevocably linked to nature, a theme that the poet cannot – does not want to – escape from, and certainly handles with his fully-fledged expertise in the field. Onomatopoeia, direct and indirect (tingle, jingle, sleigh, bells, sweet, snow, frosty, winter's), complements the poem.

A fast reading of "**To a Little Blue-Eyed Mexican Girl**" would probably make you think that it is just a tourist's chronicle. Maybe, but it is more a melancholy picture that the poet places amidst beautiful natural surroundings. Metaphors help enhance the location and the moment, interspersed with hyperboles ("eyes bluer than the clear blue sky" and "deeper than the deepest waters") and a pinch of foreignism ("Señor, Señor, por favor") as stylistic devices to bring the context closer to you. Orbach ends this genuinely sensitive poem with optimism and hope: the promise that a morning in such wondrous environment can bring something good.

I have tried myself to capture time in my writing. Orbach gives me a way to do it in this poem. In "**How to Deal with Time**" he compares time to wheels that never stop turning; yet he also comes up with a solution that is as striking as the poem itself.

The poet, like most tourists, takes photographs. "**Coyuca Lagoon**" is one; but he does not want to freeze it. He manages to hand-guide the reader with metaphors, epithets, personifications and onomatopoeia as precise expressive means aimed at producing desired effects. The onomatopoeic word "chug" is the perfect choice to oppose the two realities portrayed for the reader, "serene stillness" being on the other side. I appreciate the notion that the newly arrived are the ones absorbed by the place and the people, not the other way around: "disturbing the serene stillness with our intrusion and yet becoming one with the melody, blending quietly…". A respect to the origins and the contexts rises from these lines.

If you want to turn 180 degrees from the previous poem then go into "**Forced Freedom**". From serene places to a speeding, naked poem that exposes the poet's style to say what he thinks loudly. The poet is lured by the mirrors of the soul then defiled by the spoken word; and acts accordingly.

Orbach is touched by an instant's revelation in "**Ephemeral**". He becomes one with the "visitor" and knows they are both "sojourners in a world of hours". The poet understands their ephemeral passing through life and seeks shelter in optimism and the loveliness of things the "visitor" won't see.

Orbach brilliantly forged one piece that tells me of the cohesion among all the poems in the book: "**I Die each Evening**". Even though the poem talks about dying each evening, I am convinced this poem has a before and an afterlife in his previous and his next poems. He loves the light of day, the open spaces and nature, so he might be dying every evening; but will be reborn again tomorrow when his sun comes up.

"**Redwing**" reveals Orbach as the environmentalist and birder that he is. It shows a mature critic to the excessive and unleashed drifting of man and "civilization" from what is natural and edifying to the soul. Man is sucked in by the whirlpool of modern life and his fear to feel. Orbach fraternizes with the bird and, as a true green, wants to go to where it sings in a "softer air". I pondered long why Orbach entitled his book Redwing. When I read the poem and finished the book, I came up with my interpretation: "His conk-a-ree is a proclamation of independence; a song of freedom that begs no favours; a song that floats unchallenged…". Isn't that the poet's "decree" in his poetry? Isn't Orbach daring, martial ("Look how he shows his epaulettes"), unstoppable in his saying? That, along Orbach´s preference for those spaces the redwing covers and the bird's proud attitude ("He does not eat my offerings"), might give the readers a clue into the title if they disagree with me.

Growth and the dark roads of life. These are the ideas that come to me as I read Orbach´s "What comes of Life". He compares the smolt's fate to any person's fate. In "Chicks sent by Express" the poem is defined by the first stanza with Orbach´s critical stance.

A poem that brings to us the echoes again of an environmentalist is "**To a Butterfly**". Here is a poet in love with nature and the simple, subtle, beautiful things. Orbach contrasts the colorful butterfly with the grim world he describes to her. Once more he finds shelter in the open, in the forests and landscapes he has painted for us so many times.

"**To Mr. N— Who Does His Best in a Cartage Company**" is a tribute to a man whom the poet admires, and whose job pushes him to the utmost. "A Pine's Tree Lament" is the environmentalist's cry in a superbly woven poem. The descriptions pierce the reader's eyes and imagination. You can hear the ancient drums of alliteration in the words "branches", "brushing", "bushy". The idea that the group endures above and beyond the individual is transferred from the human to the natural world. The pine tree finds consolation in knowing its "brothers still live and endure… to drink and enjoy the ephemeral gifts of life". Despite the lament, there is recognition of life's gifts.

The poet embraces nature and the wild world around him in "**Silverfish**". It is a truly heart-felt reflection. "**True Happiness**" ends the book as a vibrant, philosophical tour-de-force. Orbach´s return to his playing with time: the yesterday-today-tomorrow labyrinth where he clings to "flashes of light".

He realizes that life brings both happiness and sadness, and seems to have discovered a stopover where he "relaxes". Somehow I modestly tried to explain that idea in a poem of mine: "We must embrace life, it carries a bag of light, a bag of darkness, both… But we must cling onto life". I can feel that in Orbach´s writing, communicated a thousand times better.

You will fly high and low with Orbach´s "blaze-of-light" Redwing. Like the bird, that takes flight or plummets to lightly touch the ground or the water, so does Orbach with his mighty verb and his sweeping descriptions in this pack of flapping poems carefully chosen by Ariella. The direct, sensitive poet has regaled us a world of movement, colors and sounds that we cannot freeze. His words are there waiting for us to open the book's pages so they can flutter and flee to Orbach's beloved nature where cormorants seem to "hold the answer to the great beyond".

Orbach's daughter has given us an outstanding compilation of her father's poetry. She put into it her love, insight and endless admiration for a man who chose to have a low profile, yet left for us a huge patrimony that shall not go unnoticed. His collecting and writing hobbies are treasures now.

Don't forget to open the book always following his instructions to Ariella when she would sit and read from his collection: "not to open the volumes too wide". Rise and glide then with the redwing, dear reader, it will be a flight to remember

M.Sc. Miguel Ángel Olivé Iglesias.
Associate Professor, University of Holguín, Cuba
President of the Canada Cuba Literary Alliance (Cuba)

Foreword

When I was a little girl, my father taught me to identify the birds common to the city and to its surrounding forests and marshes. He would impart this knowledge in the backyard or on a weekend trip to a hidden corner of the city known chiefly to birders, hoping that I too would fall in love with the gentle beauty of the birds and their song. Until today, when I see a chickadee, a cardinal, a starling or a redwing blackbird, I recall with fondness those early teachings, that most important gift my father gave me: a respect for and deep connection with the natural world of which we often forget we are a part.

Birds were one of my father's passions. The other was poetry. Growing up, the "wall of books" was a fixture in our home and in my imagination. Floor-to-ceiling, wall-to-wall, shelves were bursting with poems, a testament to the vibrancy of English-language Canadian poetry. My curiosity would lead me to randomly pick a volume off a shelf and flip through the pages until I settled into a poem that intrigued me. My father was meticulous about his collection, and I knew from early on to place each book back exactly where I found it, and never – never – open the cover too wide. Until this day, I cringe deeply whenever I see someone bend back a book's front cover.

Marvin began collecting poetry at the age of 17, beginning what was to become a lifelong passion with a copy of Montreal poet Louis Dudek's The Transparent Sea. Over the following 58 years,

Marvin's unique collection would grow to over 5,000 books, chapbooks, manuscripts and correspondence by Canadian poets writing in the English language. As my father often said, his collection was a gesture of love and appreciation for Canada and of gratitude to the country that accepted his immigrant parents from Eastern Europe. Marvin collected the writings of iconic Canadian poets like Leonard Cohen and Irving Layton, and of emerging and lesser-known poets. He would encourage and celebrate the latter by reserving them a place of equal importance in his collection. When Marvin passed away, poet Katherine L. Gordon, wrote in a tribute poem,

> *It took a genius of catalyst*
> *to blend these voices and visions:*
> *one man to appreciate and understand...*
> *give us the encouragement*
> *to see "that this was good"*
> *a movement of confidence*
> *chorus of voices blended*
> *in affirmation....*
> *we are the poets of Canada,*
> *Marvin Orbach our flag of nation,*
> *our founder, mentor, eternal emblem.*

In 2002, my father donated the wall of books that I had grown to love to the University of Calgary, where it became the Marvin Orbach Collection of Contemporary Canadian Poetry. He had explained to us that there was no question of splitting up his collection, or worse, selling it off – despite its growing monetary value. The collection was a testament to over half a century of dedication and love, and he intended that it find a home that would allow future generations to enjoy it as he had. Today, literature courses at the University of Calgary integrate the collection into their curricula. The Marvin Orbach Collection has been recognized as of "outstanding significance and national importance" by the Canadian Cultural Property Export Review Board.

Despite this unique legacy, Marvin was always very humble when approaching his vocation as a collector. Although it seemed evident to me that he bursted with pride and a sense of accomplishment at the ever-growing collection, he never bragged and he disliked being at the centre of attention. My father was one of the those rare people who was far more interested in learning about others than in talking about himself.

And so, when people asked Marvin whether he wrote poetry, his answer was always an unequivocal "no": he loved reading poetry and admired poets, but he himself was not one of them. My mother and I never thought to question this answer, and he never once spoke to us about his own writing. It was only after my father passed away in 2015, when months later my mother began sorting through his papers, that she came across an unassuming notebook hidden deep within his filing cabinet.

The poems in this book were unearthed from that filing cabinet. Some were handwritten, some typewritten and signed. Some were clearly from his university years, when he appeared to be exploring and experimenting with the styles he came across as a collector and student; others seemed to be from later, revealing a more mature, consolidated style. We can't know what his intent was for these poems, only that he kept them all those years, neatly filed in a notebook with an instruction on the cover: "Replace O'ER with OVER in these poems", written in his later years' handwriting. It was this typical meticulousness that convinced me that these poems should be shared with all who might wish to contemplate them, be moved by them, or simply sit with them.

Marvin was never comfortable in the spotlight. His pride in his lifetime accomplishments was quiet and unassuming. Yet he had a strong message to share and these poems speak of it. They speak of the destructive path that modern humanity is on, paving over everything that is alive. They speak of the power of observation, of sitting still and connecting with the life that flows around us. They speak of the joys of falling in love, and the desperation of the human condition. They speak of the simple beauty of insects, of a tree, and of course, of birds. When I look at the whole of his poems, I see in them all the lessons he taught me when I was a child, and that I carry with me and live by until today.

* * *

My father passed away in the deep cold of a February blizzard. When the snow melted and spring blew in with its warm air and first buds, a pair of cardinals appeared amidst the trees behind my home. It was the first time that I had ever seen such birds in my bustling central Montreal neighbourhood. All summer, those cardinals kept me company, and they have made an appearance every year since. I can only conclude that my father is watching over me, having finally become one with the creatures that he so loved and admired.

Ariella Orbach,
Montréal
July 2017

Introduction

I would crawl
like ants
on wild rose bushes
and watch their buds
slowly open
like the day.
I would fly
through fields
of clover after rain
and sing
to the spring sun;
spit like a snake
into the faces
of fools
who are the undoing
of what there is;
and more, to
impart
my understanding.

What is Poetry?

What is poetry my
dear pseudo-intellectual
corpses? Since I am sure
most of you haven't the
smallest idea, I shall
happily tell you.
Poetry is many things:
it is the greenness of grass;
the blueness of the sky;
the blackness of the night;
it is the twitter of
playing swallows in
the air; the shouts of
carefree children;
and all the plaintive
cooings of the doves
of human hearts.
Poetry is the softness
of down; the tenderness
of flesh; the mellow
wallowing of a tongue kiss.
Poetry is liberty;
it is ecstasy; it is
the shape of a girl's ass.

SPRING

What an Old Man Told Me

"Throw snowballs at the sun,"
he spoke.
"Shout to the wind.
Spurn men –
they mock the worm,
are play-mongers, doomed otters.
Adjust your lemur-eyes, fool:
see the maggot
gobble up your defecation.
Make friends with
the hawk;
give ear to his call.
Make your skin armour,
your form a monument."

"Better still young man,"
spoke he,
"Tear off these clownish things
and expand into a forest.
Speak to the waterfall there,
the deer and the lion.
Drink from rivers there
and greet the wary fish,
forgotten philosopher of another world.
Summon all your breath
at last, my dear friend,
spit at the laughing God."

Wishful Thinking

What?
You say you like me?
Then I like you too.

What what?
You say you wish to embrace me?
I would like that too.

What what what?
You say you wish to sleep with me?
Then let's go to it.

Initiation

Stop fussing girl; you're
not the first to feel
the gallantry of my loins.
Keep still for my energies
are assembled into one
great concourse, and I
am large-hearted. Plume
your wings and I'll
show you a crescendo of
new ideas that will
send your head a-spinning.
Or would you rather resign
like mouldering nuns to
die a sour death? Then
smile and we'll sodden
the night away, for my
assembly is fast getting
hard pressed.

Dalia

The sun is shining Dalia, on
you and me and all the world.
The death-clouds of winter
have passed, taking with them
the hardened blood from our
thawing hearts. Our veins are
bulging with fresh-flowing life,
beating out new messages to
our waking ears. We are
free now as scampering
forest-children under soft falling rain.

Let us run to our meadow where
spangled butterflies play. Laughing,
we'll chase each other round the
apple trees till we drop breathless
to the grass. Then love, my roseate
blossom, I'll imprint kisses on your
mouth your neck your shoulders and
all your honeyed parts. And when
the sun turns a flaming red, I'll
whisper into your eyes of the
many songs that were sung in
ancient times, of men and women
bound together by the blessed
ropes of love. And as the glowing
star slowly sinks into the earth
warming it with its fervent
embers, so will my heart sink
into yours, beat with yours,
live with yours, and the new
moon smiling with joy will pull
over a summer-cloud and hide her
face from our meadow and apple trees.

My Mother is the Sun

My mother is the sun
that runs in my veins,
the light that brightens
my dark eyes.

She smiles,
and the farthest
wilds of chaos
rush together
and become trees in a forest
drinking,
in quiet from the ground.

The tears of her,
that on her cheek rolls
is cool pond water, calling
to her in the swallows
of the air to look.

Like the crow
that laughs in the sky,
she is like all things bright.
She is my mother.

Victorious

Pestilent black rats
gnaw at my breast,
devour my young flesh,
rip at the freshness
of my being.

Was I born for this;
this unwanted clawing at
the soul, this poisoning
of the spirit?

No.
     Never.
I was born with
golden sunshine flowing
in my veins; sunshine-beams of love
that certainly will turn
away these devouring
vermin, blinded by
the light of life.

Golden Spring Morning on my Naked Limbs

A wreath of fruit blossoms,
blushing with spring newness
is upon my head, loosing its
sweet bouquet about my
naked limbs.

Coloured clouds are sailing by,
across the sky, raining
drops of honey on my
naked limbs.

I, walk in the wet spring
grass, can hear merry birds
chirping out spring melodies over my
naked limbs.

Bumblebees come buzzing
by me, drinking sweetness
from the air landing on my
naked limbs.

The leaves are waving at me,
Laughing and joking with the trees.
They too know spring
has returned;
she with golden trees
and golden skin;
she with mellow eyes
and golden lips; she, naked,
radiating to every hill
and valley the golden
blessings of life falls on my
naked limbs.

SUMMER

Softly Falls

Because you are a garden
I am the rain
that softly falls on you.

A Rebirth

My closed petals
open, Sabrina,
because you chose
to shine on me:
a dead flower in a dead garden
lifting my pitiful head
opening to catch
the wonder of you.

I am crying with
life, Sabrina.
Can you see my heart
begin to beat
to create
an aura of vibrant joy
enveloping the air
like a net,
drawing you to me,

to share in my song of rebirth.

A Piece of Sky

The birdbath that I bought
has given me
a piece of sky to contemplate.

For Every Damsel

She soaks herself with books of the seas
envisaging vast boundless worlds of water.
She heaves and throws with endless pleas
in the surging tides of foaming swell.
On and on she ploughs faster and faster
through the bubbling brine; the sky her sentinel.

And in the distance from out a parting cloud
flaps her harbinger, squawking shouts of glee,
soaring and dipping, announcing the news aloud.
Hearing this her turbid heart melts to dewdrops,
she espies a bowsprit streaking across the sea,
sweeping headlong coming into all her hopes.

My Love

My love,
you are the tinkle of
happy sleigh bells jingling
over the pine-sweet snow
of a frosty winter's morn.

My love,
you are the song of a
warbling vireo floating lazily
on the gentle spring wind
kissing every leaf as you pass.

My love,
you are the voice of a
bubbling brook laughing your
way down a mountain slope
filling the summer air with merriment.

My love,
you are the murmur of an
autumn wood treading the
forest floor whispering your
news to visiting creatures.

To a Little Blue-Eyed Mexican Girl

Now while I wait here on this
far-stretching beach, camera in hand,
ready to capture the vast Pacific
sunset in all its splendour,
you approach me, little girl, sweet
innocence. You compliment the
very sand you walk over as your
dainty little toes sink into its
brown richness, giving every tiny
grain moments of joy. Your long
black curls play about your
shoulders in carefree merriment.
Your eyes are holy treasures to behold;
bluer than a clear blue sky, deeper
than the deepest waters. They shine
gently on me little girl, but only
with sadness. Your tattered clothes cannot
hide your sun-browned skin;
your countenance glows like
the sun that is setting now on the distant
horizon, shedding its rich beauty
on me, drowning me in your delight.

"Señor, Señor. Por favor."
You ask me to buy some shells
you gathered along the shore;
shells that perhaps might please my eye.

Little girl, your voice is filled with
a sadness, far sadder that the
darkening waves rolling
over the soft sand shore.
Come. Give me your little hand and we
will walk along the beach under the
crimson sky. We'll walk on the warm
sand and I'll tell you of the cheer
the morning might bring.

How to Deal with Time

With wheels of rubber
rolling down darkening
hills never stopping –
where do minutes and seconds
go, to melt into black
valleys of yesterday?

But we, girl, can
slash the bedeviled
orbs with that arrow
that fell from the sky.

Coyuca Lagoon

Chugging slowly over
gentle dark waves
disturbing the serene
stillness with our intrusion
and yet becoming one
with the melody,
blending quietly,
a new sound already
an old actor in this
ancient drama.

Startled egrets lift
into the air
fluttering excitedly
then settling again.
Near the shore, little
tanned children bob
in the water, playing
ancient games of laughter
peacefully, letting their
sun-soaked limbs swing
freely with the element.

Behind them an array
of coconut palms, tall
with majestic pride,
their fronds drunk
with the soft sweet air,
wave gently in the wind.
Ahead, a large
forbidding mangrove, silent
with mystery. Secretive
cormorants flying swiftly by
seeming to hold the
answers to the great beyond.

Beams of sky shimmer
across the still water
chasing each other,
dancing with happiness,
teasing my inebriated eyes.
From afar the solitary
splash of a diving pelican
reaches my ears.

Chugging and chugging,
onward into this
never-ending drama,
onward deep into the
shadows of the
living lagoon,
onward till my curtain falls.

Forced Freedom

When you look at
me with those soft-glinting
eyes and tender-parting
lips my heart's blood
rises like mercury on
a hot summer day,
but when you speak,
dyspeptic wench, it
falls like a finished
erection happy to be free.

AUTUMN

Ephemeral

Sitting by a moon-lit lake,
thinking of wasted days gone by
and of the quiet wavelets that
endlessly lick at the shore,
you appear out of the air in
midnight raiment and alight
on my nose. Startled by the
intrusion I am about to flick
you away, but no I cannot.
You tickle my nose as no lover
can and I like the feel of
your tiny feet.

Alas, we are both but
sojourners in a world of
hours, clinging desperately
to our mysterious beings.
How many struggling years
were you in the dark of the
womb, only to be born now
under the glow of a feeble
moon? O Life, you enter
unreasonable palpitating with
delusion and fade away like
the dying light of day.
Visitor, stay here with me
yet a while. The night is
dark and it's a hostile world.
I shall tell you of the rising
sun you will not see, and of
the green of the fields and blue
of the sky. Visitor, spend with me
your last uneventful minutes,
for I am one who understands.

I Die Each Evening

I die each evening
with the setting sun.
When the sun melts
in its last splash of life
I die,
I melt
with the agony of beauty
into that death-moment
of darkness, when
the folding flowers
call
from every garden
of my soul.

Redwing

Most city people are stupid;
of that I am sure. They would
scare away that redwing that sings
at this moment in my poplar tree.
Look how he shows his epaulettes;
a fresher red I have never seen.
His conk-a-ree is a proclamation
of independence; a song of freedom
that begs no favours; a song
that floats unchallenged in a
decaying city, deaf in both ears.
I love this bird, with a love
that is beyond love. He does not
eat my offerings, and still he
comes, bringing his cooling
marsh aromas. I drink to you
friend, with a heart that is
now lighter. But before you
leave for your nest among the
cattails, tell me that one
day I may come to you, and
together we'll sing in a
softer air.

What Comes of Life

Once happy,
splashing and racing
in crystal pools
of joy;
now a little smolt,
slim and silver
and strong for
adventure,
swimming down
ominous corridors
with a dirty
sea for an
end.

Chicks Sent by Express Train

Callous world,
world of contracting emotions,
world that reeks
of unintelligence,
world of wisdom
I address you
not with words, but
with the foul wind
that blows from an
ill-twisted mouth.

Watch these cartons of
frightened little chicks,
motherless creations
peeping with terror midst
horrendous engines screaming
their black servitude.

Little balls of breath,
uniting and lifting into
the confused air, their
own symphony of
questions, a chorus of
living inquiry blackened
and turned away by
the very air that hears,
unheard, unanswered, alone.

To a Butterfly

Sylvan jewel, pride of the
alluring wood, you are lost.
What do you do here in this
place of walking cadavers?
What possible scent could
have drawn you to this colourless
corner? Your powdery buffs
have no business in my garden
of weeds. You flaunt me. Your
dappled wings are tearing at
my soul; pinching my gaunt
face. You'll find no nectar
here, save that which is
painted on haggard harlots.
Away with you. Away from
this cacophonous grave of
confusion. Fly back to your
honeyed realm of sweet smelling
blossoms; back to where
chipmunks still scamper about
and fill the forest with their
merry innocence. Leave me now,
for I am prisoner of a dying race.

To Mr. N—
Who Does His Best in a Cartage Company

My bantam friend,
I praise your endeavours.
Keep up the good work.
Carry your little body with
worthy pride and let not
the noisy week weigh you down.
Running along the conveyor belt
dodging the moving boxes
you shout out
your resounding commands
like a little Napoleon
to the broad-shouldered
men below you,
prodding them on
with unrelenting cusses.
Your whole five-foot
frame is chock-full of
undying energy and
your mere presence
glistens with incentive.
A lasting tribute to you.

A Pine Tree's Lament

There are still my brothers who
stretch high into the tranquil air,
washing the spaces with their
living song, but I am fallen crippled,
severed at the knees, to lie
upon the ancient soil and die
a tortured death.

My once-bending boughs now
cover a weedy field, crying like
dying eagles in the slums of their
empire. The earth is taking me back,
swallowing me in its black clutches,
slowly eating my perfumed flanks.

And all this from that new arrival,
highest of egotists, who came swinging
his savage axe to disturb the forest
with his brain. Soon perhaps I'll be
food for his domestic onions. Oh, how
I once towered with pleasure, quietly
swaying with perfect grace, shaming
the swans that float in the lake.

Squirrels chased all day on my proud
branches, tickling me gently, brushing
my chest with their bushy tails.
Shining blackbirds came to me too,
and sparrows and robins to rest in my
shade. But that is gone; I am no more.

Already the earth is about me, and I
can feel the worms, those horrible
inevitable worms, so soft and yet so final.
A curse upon mankind! He stopped me
in my prime, in my wonderful prime,
when all the world was sharing the
nectar of my cones, the truth that sped
like a bird to all my neighbours.

And now I am half devoured by my
own mother's womb, a young Adonis,
just beginning and just finishing,
ending as nourishment for my assassin's
stinking onions. Oh the misery of it!
But my brothers still live and endure,
if only for a while, to drink and enjoy
the ephemeral gifts of life.

WINTER

Silverfish

Flee away silverfish,
I'm trying to write a poem.
Flee away silverfish,
or I'm sure to crush you.

I walk as an old man
with sorrows for my cane,
and yet I am young.
I am weak with life's injuries.

As a foot fallen asleep,
so am I, paralyzed and numbed
by days made bleak.

I hear laughter breaking,
echoing from happy summers
of my youth. But I am old,
and the wind is blowing cold.

Flee away silverfish,
or your darting here and there
will be the end of you.

I am tired of looking into
mirrors and peering at my crusty
face, tired of straightening my
hair and walking on cold sidewalks
that make me swim in false hopes.

I know there are flower petals
falling on my head. But my arms
hang lifeless at my sides,
too heavy to rise and gather
them before my eyes.

There's a fragrance emanating
from them, but I cannot see them at all.
A fragrance that tells of spring
and birds and butterflies.

Play on silverfish,
you make good company for one
such as me, and I wouldn't
have it otherwise.

Perhaps the morning sun will break
the window and gild my chest,
and all the petals will tumble
down into my hands.

True Happiness

Yesterday it was dark,
far darker than the darkest night,
and I was not.
Today I am, and there is light,
occasional flashes like lightening
in a black storm,
illuminating the darkness,
then leaving.
I sing and cry until I am tired,
for I am.
I sleep and wake,
and yet see the darkness,
for I have eyes that like a pond
reflect the night.
The flashes that I perceive
are telltale;
they show me a greater darkness
than yesterday.
But they are flashes,
and I am,
and so I cry and sing
and do what becomes myself,
till I am no more.
And tomorrow when I am no more,
it will be as dark as yesterday,
without flashes of light
to prod and pinch my being.

Today I am happy and sad,
for I am what I am.
But tomorrow I shall relax
and be happiest
for I will not be.

A Short Biography of Marvin Orbach

Marvin Orbach was born in 1940 in Toronto to Bella and Carl Orbach, who had arrived from Poland in the 1920s. Marvin moved to Montreal with his parents and brother Bernie at the age of 12. After obtaining a Masters in Library Science from McGill University in 1966, Orbach channeled his love of learning and of literature into a 39-year career as a reference and selections librarian at Concordia University. In 1974 he married Gabriella Singerman, a contemporary ballet dancer and teacher who, in 1982, gave birth to their daughter Ariella.

Orbach began collecting English-language poetry books at 17 years of age. From his first acquisition, Montreal poet Louis Dudek's The Transparent Sea, until Orbach's death in 2015, his unique collection grew to over 5,000 books, chapbooks, manuscripts and correspondence by Canadian poets writing in the English language. Orbach collected the works and ephemera of iconic Canadian poets – Leonard Cohen, Irving Layton – and of emerging and lesser-known poets, whom he encouraged and celebrated by reserving them a space of equal importance in his collection.

For decades, Orbach's collection grew in his home in Montreal. In 2002, he donated his 2,400 books and ephemera to the University of Calgary, where it became the Marvin Orbach Collection of Contemporary Canadian Poetry. When Orbach retired in 2005, he began adding to his collection weekly, more than doubling its size between 2002 and 2015. The Marvin Orbach Collection is recognized as cultural property of national importance by the Canadian Cultural Property Export Review Board. The collection, Orbach has explained, was motivated by his love for Canada and his gratitude for the country's acceptance of his immigrant parents.

Aside from poetry, Marvin cultivated a passion for travel, visiting such far-ranging places as the jungles of Peru and Brazil, the former Yugoslavia and the Israeli desert; he worked and studied Hebrew on a kibbutz for one year after graduating from his Bachelors degree at McGill University. Orbach was also a dedicated birder and environmentalist who often described his "religion" as a that of a deep love and connection with nature. These themes are pervasive in his poetry.

Marvin Orbach died on February 8, 2015, at the age of 74. He was adding volumes to his collection until his final days. Known to be a very modest person, Orbach never told anyone about his own poems, which were found after his passing by his wife Gabriella. On his tombstone is an inscription from one of his muses, Leonard Cohen: There's a blaze of light | In every word.

www.ingramcontent.com/pod-product-compliance
Lightning Source LLC
LaVergne TN
LVHW090039080526
838202LV00046B/3876